curious about

BULL SHARKS

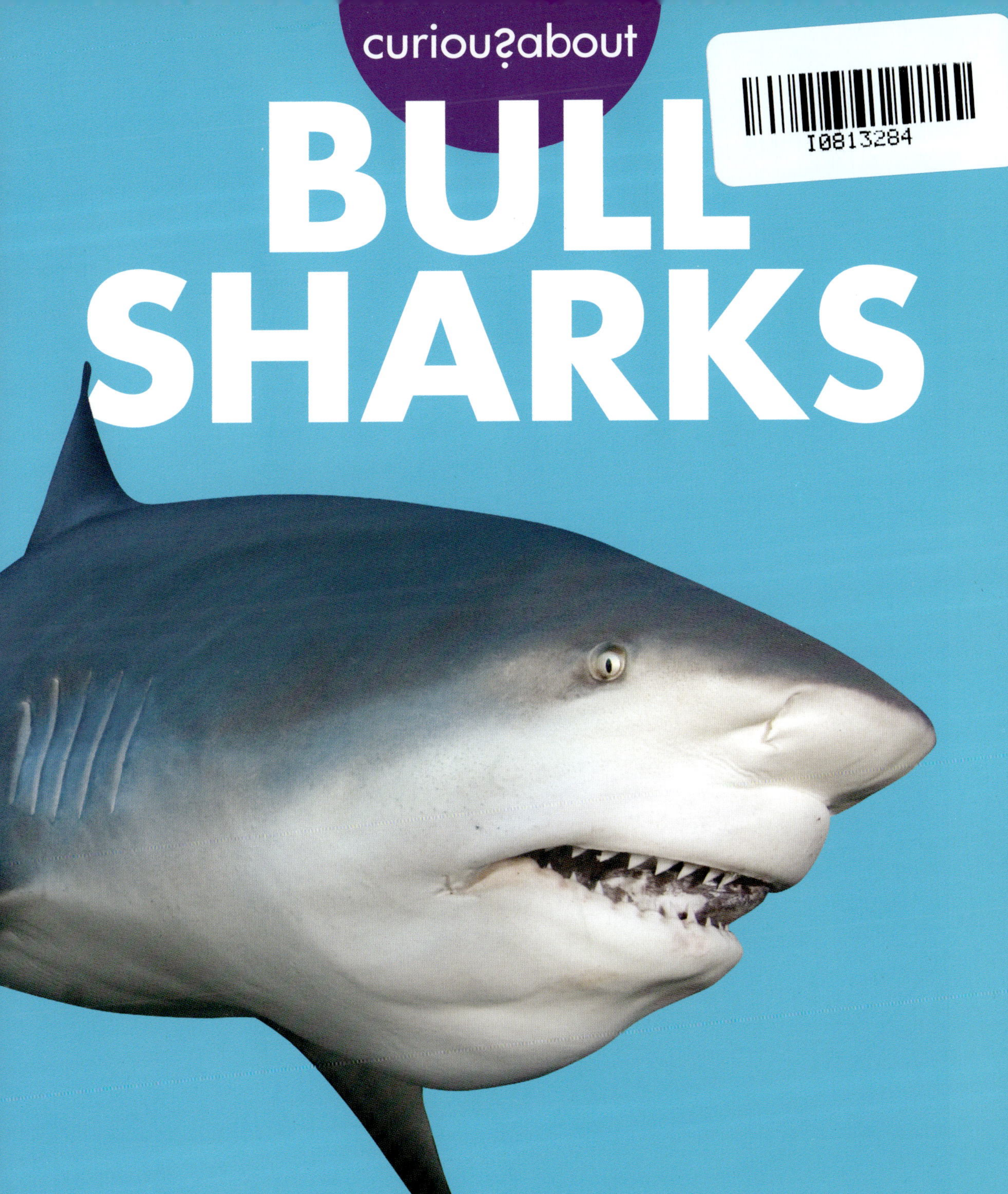

BY EMMA ALICE JOHNSON

AMICUS LEARNING

I0813284

What are you

curious about?

CHAPTER THREE

Life in the Ocean

Curious About is published by
Amicus Learning, an imprint of Amicus
P.O. Box 227, Mankato, MN 56002
www.amicuspublishing.us

Copyright © 2026 Amicus.
International copyright reserved in all countries.
No part of this book may be reproduced in any form without written permission from the publisher.

Editor: Ana Brauer
Series Designer: Kathleen Petelinsek
Book Designer and Photo Researcher: Sara Hood

Library of Congress Cataloging-in-Publication Data
Names: Johnson, Emma (Emma Alice), author.
Title: Curious about bull sharks / Emma Alice Johnson.
Description: Mankato, MN : Amicus Learning, an imprint of Amicus, [2026] | Series: Curious about sharks | Includes bibliographical references and index. | Audience: Ages 6–9 | Audience: Grades 2–3 | Summary: "Can bull sharks live in lakes? Learn about these strong ocean animals in this question-and-answer book for elementary-aged readers. Includes infographics, table of contents, glossary, books and websites for further research, and index"— Provided by publisher.
Identifiers: LCCN 2024048308 (print) | LCCN 2024048309 (ebook) | ISBN 9798892005036 (library binding) | ISBN 9798892005579 (paperback) | ISBN 9798892006118 (ebook)
Subjects: LCSH: Bull shark—Juvenile literature.
Classification: LCC QL638.95.C3 J64 2026 (print) | LCC QL638.95.C3 (ebook) | DDC 597.3/4—dc23/eng/20241207
LC record available at https://lccn.loc.gov/2024048308
LC ebook record available at https://lccn.loc.gov/2024048309

Photo Credits: Alamy Stock Photo/David Fleetham, 2, 9, 3, 17, George Karbus Photography, 18–19, Jeff Rotman, 8, Michael Patrick O'Neill, cover, 1, Mike Greenslade/Australia, 4–5; Getty Images/Alastair Pollock Photography, 10–11, Reinhard Dirscherl/ullstein bild, 6–7, Rodrigo Friscione, 12, 2, 13; Shutterstock/Alexander Machulskiy, 20–21, Orion Media Group, 15; The Noun Project/Arkinasi, 22, IronSV, 23, sandra, 22, 23; Vecteezy/om1947, 16

Printed in India

CHAPTER ONE

Why are they called bull sharks?

Remora fish attach themselves to bull sharks. They eat scraps left over by the shark.

DID YOU KNOW?
Bull sharks have many other names. In Africa they are called Zambi!

These sharks are named after bulls. Bulls are tough animals. They like headbutting. Bull sharks have short, strong snouts. They use them to headbutt their food. A bull shark has dark gray skin on top. Its belly is white. These sharks are **aggressive** animals.

Do bull sharks swim in groups?

Not often. Bull sharks are loners. They usually live and hunt alone. But sometimes, two bull sharks will hunt together. They have a bond that lasts over time. This might be called friendship. Bull sharks also gather in groups during **mating** season.

Bull sharks will sometimes hunt in small groups.

Do bull sharks remember things?

Yes! Bull sharks can remember other sharks. They also remember their favorite food spot. Scientists found that bull sharks always came back to an area for food. Even when years passed and there was no food, they still remembered it. They came back when there was food.

DID YOU KNOW?

Scientists often put tags on sharks. These let them track where the sharks go.

Bull sharks often remember and return to the same locations they have been before.

CHAPTER TWO

How do bull sharks hunt?

Remora Fish

Bull sharks can sense a fish's movement in the water.

Bull sharks mostly hunt alone. Sometimes they hunt with a friend. They use a ram-and-bite attack. They swim at their **prey** fast. Then they ram into it. This stuns the animal. Then the bull shark bites the prey.

How strong is their bite?

While it is not recommended to feed sharks, some divers are trained to do so.

Bull sharks have a strong bite. They have powerful jaw muscles. Their bite is stronger than any other shark their size. They even have a stronger bite than a same-sized great white shark! That is how they eat big meals.

DID YOU KNOW?
Bull sharks can grow to be up to 11 feet (3.4 meters) long. This is about the size of a male great white shark.

Bull sharks also have a strong tail. It lets them swim quickly.

What do bull sharks eat?

A lot of things! They are not picky eaters. They mostly eat fish. Sometimes they will eat big animals like dolphins, sea turtles, and sea lions. They might even eat dead animals or other sharks!

Bull sharks will eat almost any animal they come across.

Where do bull sharks live?

Most bull sharks live in the ocean. They mostly live in warm water by the coast. Sometimes they live in rivers. They hunt in waters where people swim. This means they are more dangerous than other sharks.

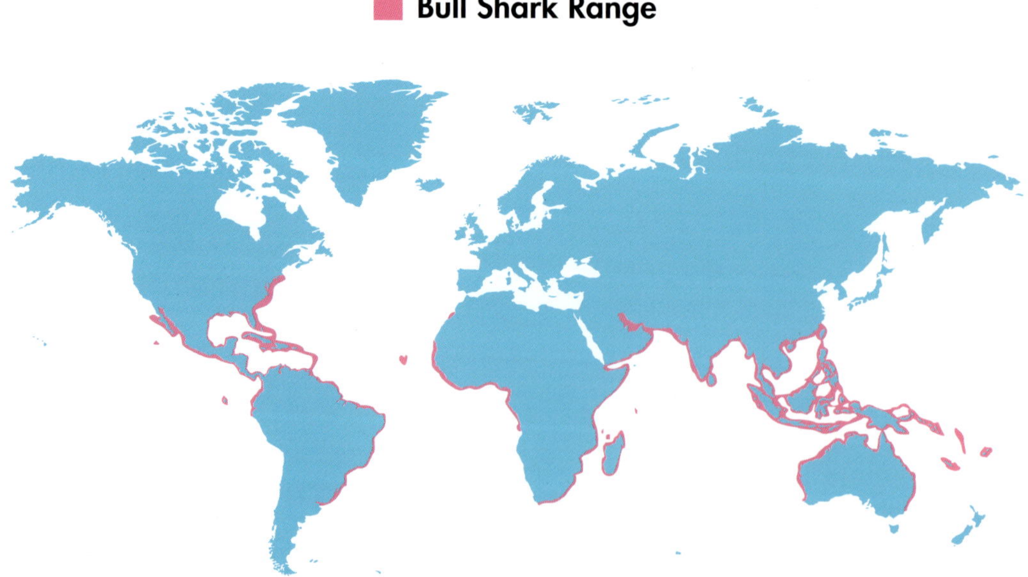

While bull sharks are more aggressive than others, shark attacks are very rare.

DID YOU KNOW?
Bull sharks were once found on a golf course. They were in a river that flooded. Then they swam to a lake on a golf course!

Can bull sharks live in lakes?

Yes. They can live in **salt water** or **fresh water**. No other shark can live in both! All sharks need salt water. Bull sharks can hold salt in their bodies. That is how they can survive in a river or lake.

Bull sharks have a lifespan of 12 to 16 years.

Do bull sharks sleep?

They do not sleep like people do. Sometimes they do not move. They slow down and rest. Some scientists think this might be sleeping. Bull sharks cannot stop moving for long. They need to keep moving to breathe.

Bull sharks often sleep with their eyes open.

ASK MORE QUESTIONS

What is special about bull shark teeth?

How far do bull sharks travel?

Try a BIG QUESTION: How do bull sharks help keep the ocean healthy?

SEARCH FOR ANSWERS

Search the library catalog or the Internet.
A librarian, teacher, or parent can help you.

Using Keywords
Find the looking glass.

Keywords are the most important words in your question.

If you want to know about:

- bull shark teeth, type: BULL SHARK TEETH
- how far bull sharks travel, type: BULL SHARK LOCATIONS

LEARN MORE

FIND GOOD SOURCES

Here are some good, safe sources you can use in your research.
Your librarian can help you find more.

Books

Bull Sharks
by Rachel Rose, 2022.

Bull Sharks
by Rebecca Pettiford, 2021.

Internet Sites

National Geographic Kids | Bull Sharks
https://kids.nationalgeographic.com/animals/fish/facts/bull-shark
National Geographic Society is one of biggest science groups in the world. They make *National Geographic* magazine.

Ocean Conservancy | Bull Sharks
https://oceanconservancy.org/wildlife-factsheet/bull-shark/
Ocean Conservancy works to keep bull sharks and other ocean life safe.

Every effort has been made to ensure that these websites are appropriate for children. However, because of the nature of the Internet, it is impossible to guarantee that these sites will remain active indefinitely or that their contents will not be altered.

SHARE AND TAKE ACTION

Make a model of a bull shark with clay.
Remember the short snout!

Draw a picture of a bull shark tooth.
How is it different than your teeth?

Help take care of the oceans for bull sharks.
Join a beach clean-up.

GLOSSARY

aggressive Showing a readiness to fight or attack.

fresh water Naturally occurring water that is not salty and is suitable for drinking if cleaned. Lakes and rivers are fresh water.

mate When two animals get together to produce young.

prey An animal hunted or killed for food.

salt water Naturally occurring water that has salt in it. The ocean is salt water.

INDEX

About the Author

Emma Alice Johnson lives on a farm in the woods. She grows flowers and loves insects. Bumblebees are her favorite insects. She is friends with a cat, a pig, and a bunch of chickens. She once swam with nurse sharks!